Cambridge Primary

Hodder Cambridge Primary
English

Activity Book
C

Foundation Stage

Ruth Price

HODDER
EDUCATION
AN HACHETTE UK COMPANY

Acknowledgements

Every effort has been made to trace all copyright holders, but if any have been inadvertently overlooked the Publishers will be pleased to make the necessary arrangements at the first opportunity.

Text credits

p.22 The poem *Zola has a zoo…* adapted from '*I want…*' by Wes Magee with kind permission from Wes Magee.

Hachette UK's policy is to use papers that are natural, renewable and recyclable products and made from wood grown in well-managed forests and other controlled sources. The logging and manufacturing processes are expected to conform to the environmental regulations of the country of origin.

Orders: please contact Bookpoint Ltd, 130 Milton Park, Abingdon, Oxon OX14 4SB. Telephone: (44) 01235 827720. Fax: (44) 01235 400454. Lines are open from 9.00–5.00, Monday to Saturday, with a 24-hour message answering service. You can also order through our website www.hoddereducation.com

Published by Hodder Education

An Hachette UK Company

Carmelite House, 50 Victoria Embankment, London EC4Y 0DZ

Impression number   5 4 3 2

Year   2023 2022 2021 2020

Cover illustrations by Steve Evans

Illustrations by Vian Oelofsen

Typeset in FS Albert Regular 17/19 pt by Lizette Watkiss

Printed in India

A catalogue record for this title is available from the British Library

978 1 5104 5726 3

MiX
Paper from
responsible sources
FSC™ C104740

Contents

Sequencing

We use these words to say things in order:

| first | then | next | last |

For example, to draw a fish:

First, draw a triangle.

Then draw an arrowhead next to it.

Next, draw an eye and a mouth.

Last, draw a pattern.

⭐ Name the animals. Say how to draw each animal in just four steps. Use these words:

| first | then | next | last |

bird

lion

⭐ Choose another animal. Draw it in just four steps.

1.

2.

3.

4.

⭐ Say how to draw your animal. Use these words:

| first | then | next | last |

Story steps

⭐ The story below is muddled up. Number each picture in the correct order.

How Bear lost his tail

I have
no tail!

You can catch
fish with your
tail too.

⭐ Retell the story using the words below.

In the beginning   The next day   And so   Finally   And that

Draw your own five-step story sequence.

1. In the beginning …

2. The next day …

3. And so …

4. Finally …

5. And that …

 Tell your story to a friend.

In the beginning …

Matching story endings

⭐ Join each story to its ending.

Story A	Story B	Story C

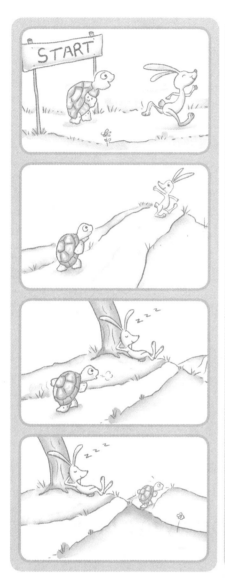

⭐ Tick the story ending you like best. Tell the story to a friend.

How questions

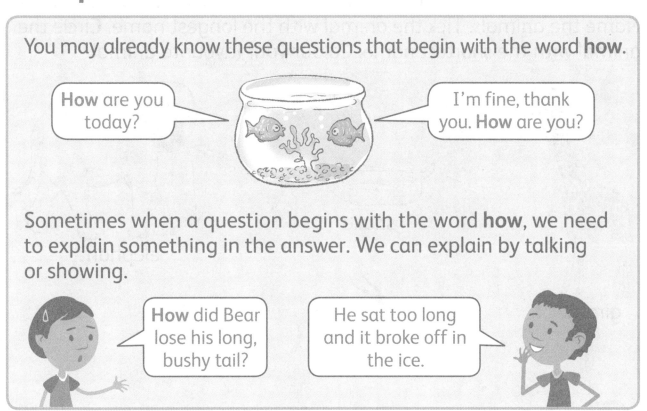

You may already know these questions that begin with the word **how**.

> **How** are you today?

> I'm fine, thank you. **How** are you?

Sometimes when a question begins with the word **how**, we need to explain something in the answer. We can explain by talking or showing.

> **How** did Bear lose his long, bushy tail?

> He sat too long and it broke off in the ice.

⭐ Ask yourself these questions. Circle the answer.

How do I feel today?	🙂 😐 🙁

How many bees can I see?		5 6 7

How much do I like animals?	not much a little a lot

⭐ Say a **how** question. Ask a friend to answer.

Word families: animals

⭐ Name the animals. Tick the animal with the longest name. Circle the animal with the shortest name. Colour your favourite animal.

giraffe

snake

elephant

antelope

lion

eagle

cheetah

zebra

crocodile

rhinoceros

tiger

Find and circle these words in the wordsearch:

ant

frog

panda

bat

kangaroo

zebra

owl

flamingo

Tips:
Look this way from left to right.

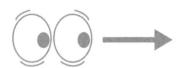

Look across and down.

Look down.

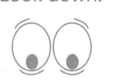

f	r	o	g	a	o	b	a
c	l	d	g	k	w	l	n
m	b	a	t	n	l	p	t
q	z	s	m	t	u	k	g
v	e	i	w	i	m	x	t
a	b	o	p	a	n	d	a
n	r	f	d	u	b	g	a
k	a	n	g	a	r	o	o

11

Describing words

When we want to tell about how something looks, we describe it.
We can use colour words.
We can use words about size and pattern.

a big blue spotty elephant

 Colour each animal to match its caption. Tick the big animals. Circle the little animals.

a big brown bear

a big grey elephant

a little orange monkey

a little green lizard

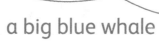

a little yellow fish

a big blue whale

⭐ Join the animals that are similar. Say how. Use these words:

| spots | stripes | horns | wings | fur |

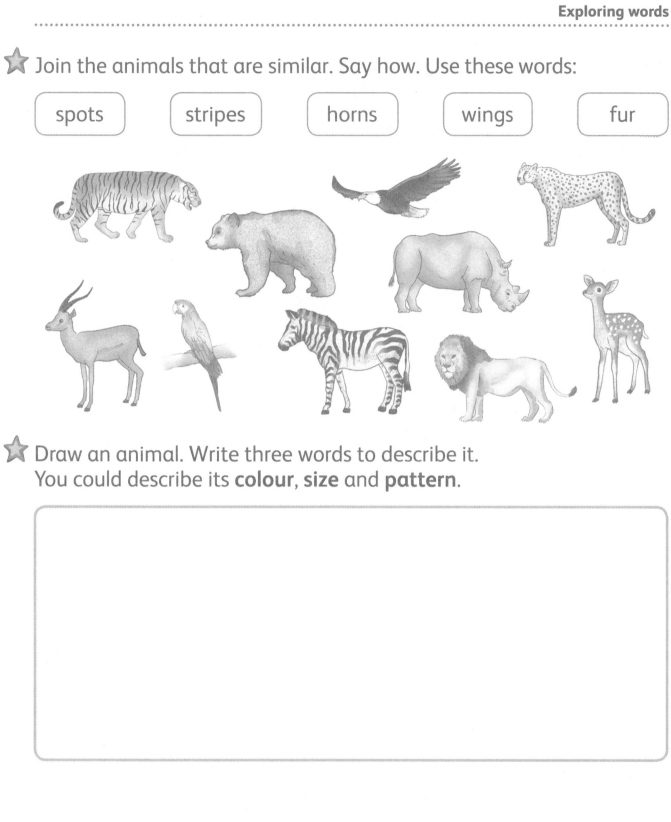

⭐ Draw an animal. Write three words to describe it.
You could describe its **colour**, **size** and **pattern**.

_____

_____

_____

Animals of the future

Some animals looked like this in the past.

What do you think animals will look like in the future?

 Create a new animal of the future.
1. Draw two animals you like.
2. Circle what you think is best about each animal.
3. Use the best bits to draw a new animal of the future.
4. Label it.

My new animal

⭐ What is your new animal's name?

_____

⭐ Tell more about your new animal. Tick the correct answer.

	Yes	No
Does it have a plain coat?	☐	☐
Is it big?	☐	☐
Does it have wings?	☐	☐
Is it spotty?	☐	☐
Does it have fur?	☐	☐
Is it just one colour?	☐	☐
Does it live in the sea?	☐	☐
Is it friendly?	☐	☐
Does it help humans?	☐	☐
Can it speak?	☐	☐

⭐ Describe your animal to a friend.

Using voice

You can use your voice in different ways.
It can be **loud** or **soft**. It can be **high** or **low**.

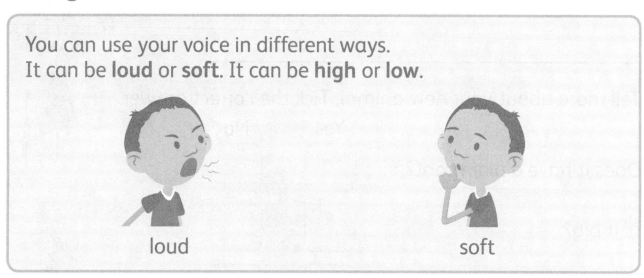

loud   soft

⭐ Look at the pictures. Write ⬡S⬡ if you would use a **soft** voice.

Write ⬡L⬡ if you would use a **loud** voice.

⭐ Draw a place where you must use a soft voice.

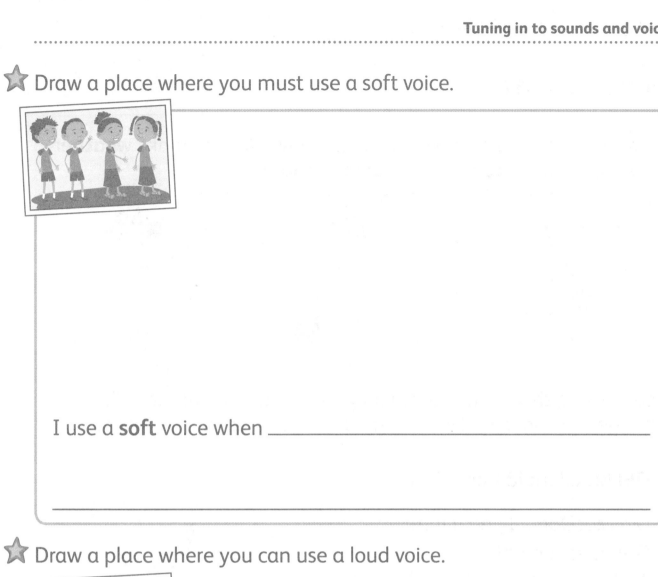

I use a **soft** voice when _____

_____

⭐ Draw a place where you can use a loud voice.

I use a **loud** voice when _____

_____

Voice sounds

We can use voice sounds in different ways. We can make **weather sounds**, **transport sounds** or **animal sounds**.

pitter patter

brrum, brrum

cluck, cluck

⭐ Read or sing this rhyme together and make the animal sounds. Change the underlined words for each animal picture and its sound.

Old Macdonald had a farm

Old MacDonald had a farm,
Ee-igh-ee-igh-oh!
And on that farm he had some <u>chickens</u>,
Ee-igh-ee-igh-oh!

With a <u>cluck-cluck</u> here,
And a <u>cluck-cluck</u> there,
Here a <u>cluck</u>, there a <u>cluck</u>,
Everywhere a <u>cluck-cluck</u>,

Old MacDonald had a farm,
Ee-igh-ee-igh-oh!

meh-meh

gobble-gobble

quack-quack

neigh-neigh (say nay-nay)

18

⭐ Now you choose an animal and its sound to add to the rhyme. Write the words in each gap.

Old MacDonald had a farm,

Ee-igh-ee-igh-oh!

And on that farm he had some

_____,

Ee-igh-ee-igh-oa!

With a _____ here,

And a _____ there,

Here a _____, there a _____,

Everywhere a _____,

Old MacDonald had a farm,

Ee-igh-ee-igh-oh!

Repeating letter sounds in words

In some rhymes we repeat sounds and words.

We can repeat letter sounds at the beginning of words too.

The (b)rave (b)ug (b)it the (b)ig (b)ear.

 Read this sentence together.

Circle all the letter | l | s.

Lions like to lick lovely lemon lollipops.

Now say the sentence again and again.
How fast can you go and still say the words?

 Draw something that begins with the same letter sound.
Write its name.

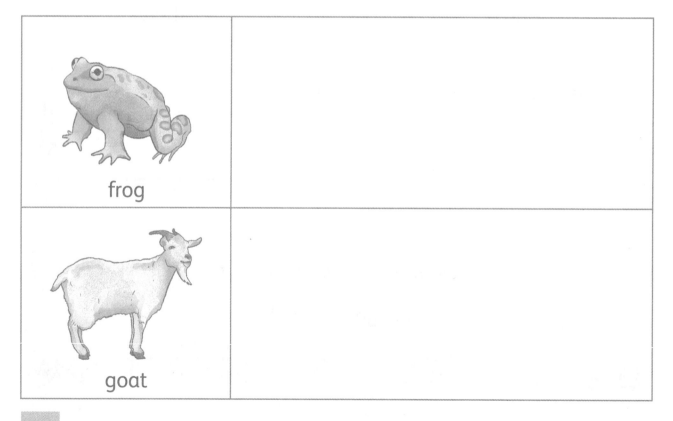

frog	
goat	

Name the animals. Join the animals that begin with the same letter sound.

lion

tiger

penguin

turtle

peacock

raccoon

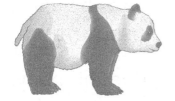

panda

leopard

hamster

horse

lizard

rabbit

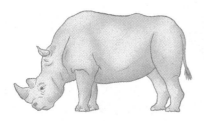

rhino

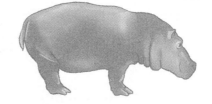

hippo

toucan

Repeating letter sounds in rhymes

⭐ Read this rhyme together.
Circle the words that begin with the same letters.

Zola has a zoo …

Ravi owns a rabbit,

Rowan gets a rat,

Lulu wants a lizard,

But me?

I want a bat!

Bina loves her birds,

Dani walks her dog,

Ping rides his pony,

But me?

I want a frog!

Hari has a hamster,

Cari's cats mew,

Sajid strokes his snake,

But me?

I am Zola and

I HAVE A ZOO!

Write your name and an animal name that begins with the same letter sound.

 Zara – Zebra

 Tick the picture that begins with the same letter sound as the animal name to make a funny phrase.

 a parrot in pyjamas

a shark in a

a tiger in a

a hippo in a

Phoneme spotting

Sometimes two or three letters make one sound:

(ar) (or) (ur) (ow) (oi) (er) (ear) (air)

c**ar**   f**or**k   c**ur**l   **ow**l

c**oi**n   flow**er**   b**ear**d   h**air**

 Say the word for each picture.

Tick things with the sound (ear). Circle things with the sound (air).

hair   beard   ear

earrings   pair of shoes   tear

⭐ Circle the letters that are in the word for the picture.

ar   er   ur   or   ow   oi

er   ow   ow   or   ur   ar

or   er   oi   ur   ow   oi

⭐ Play *Snakes and Ladders.*
This is a game for two players.

Things you need:

Spin the spinner. Read the word.

If you land on a snake, you slip back down. If you land on a ladder, you zoom up!

counters   spinner

20. sh-or-t	21. c-ar	22. h-ear	23. w-i-nn-er	Finish
19. n-ow	18. h-air	17. ow-l	16. t-ur-n	15. d-ar-k
10. n-or-th	11. sh-ar-k	12. ch-air	13. r-i-v-er	14. f-air
9. p-or-ch	8. f-ar-m-er	7. p-air	6. n-ear	5. j-oi-n
Start	1. p-ar-k	2. c-or-k	3. f-ur	4. d-ow-n

Reading and spelling words

Consonant letters are:

b, c, d, f, g, h, j, k, l, m, n, p, q, r, s, t, v, w, x, y and Z.

Sometimes words begin with two consonant letters.

Sometimes words end with two consonant letters.

<u>fr</u>og (f)-(r)-(o)-(g)   po<u>nd</u> (p)-(o)-(n)-(d)

Each letter has its own sound. We blend each sound in the word to read it.

⭐ Add a dot under each letter. Blend each sound to read the word. Join each word to its matching picture.

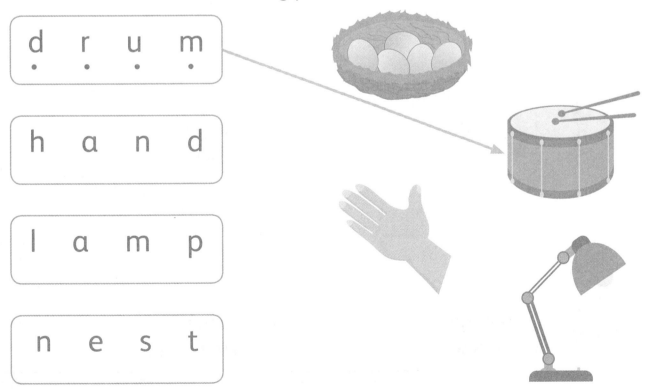

d r u m

h a n d

l a m p

n e s t

Read and write the word chains.

slip → change **i** to **o** → slop → change **l** to **t** → stop

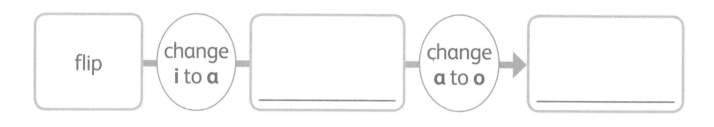

flip → change **i** to **a** → ___ → change **a** to **o** → ___

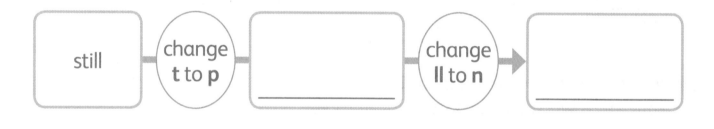

still → change **t** to **p** → ___ → change **ll** to **n** → ___

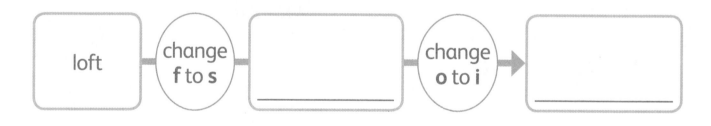

loft → change **f** to **s** → ___ → change **o** to **i** → ___

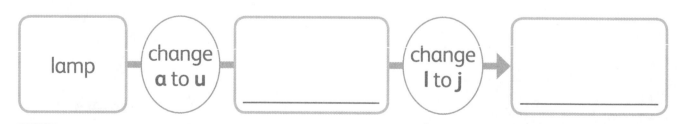

lamp → change **a** to **u** → ___ → change **l** to **j** → ___

Tricky words

Some words are tricky to read. Try to read them in these groups.

| said | have | like | some | come |

| were | there | when | what |

| so | do | little | one | out |

⭐ Read the little story. Find the tricky words below and circle them.

| were | one | some | what | do |

| there | said | so | little | like |

Playing in the woods

We were playing in the woods.

'What shall we do now?' I said.

'Let's get some wood. Let's make

a den over there,' said Ali.

So Ali got a big log and I got a

little one.

We like it in the woods.

Read the sentences. Fill each gap with a tricky word below.

said   have

like   come

what   one

We _____ the box was a rocket.

When shall we go to the Moon?

We _____ to go now.

_____ on, let's **do** it!

_____ will we see **there**?

We may see a **little** monster.

I hope we see a big _____.

I _____ monsters.

Well, I like **some** monsters!

Sorting pretend or real

There are lots of different kinds of stories.
Some stories tell about real life. Some stories tell about pretending.

Real: Zack goes to school.

Pretend: Mina on the Moon.

⭐ Sort the real and pretend stories. Join each book to a shelf.

Draw a cover for a real story.

 What is the story about?

_____

_____

_____

Draw a cover for a pretend story.

 What is the story about?

_____

_____

_____

Choosing an ending

⭐ Read the sentences. Tick the ending you like best.

The Tortoise and the Hare

Tortoise and Hare were running. Both wanted to win.

Hare was winning so he took a nap.

or

Tortoise took a nap too.

Tortoise ran past Hare and won the race.

⭐ Tell a friend why you like that ending best.

Read the sentences. Draw and write what you think happens next.

(1) The children were looking at a pretend dinosaur swamp.

(2) Flash! They were in Dinosaur Land! They looked up to see a T-Rex right over them.

(3)

_____

_____

_____

_____

_____

Reading sentences

⭐ Read the sentences. Join each sentence to its matching picture.

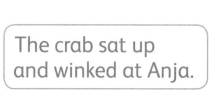
Vikram and Anna were making things for the fair.

The crab sat up and winked at Anja.

It was a good day for sailing.

The six little monsters were waiting for the bus.

It was haircut day and Ben was cross.

'Let's catch some fish and shells,' said Jess.

The little doll set sail in her boat.

'I am off to the Moon in my rocket!' said Ashraf.

⭐ Tick the sentences above that pretend.

⭐ Say three sentences that pretend.

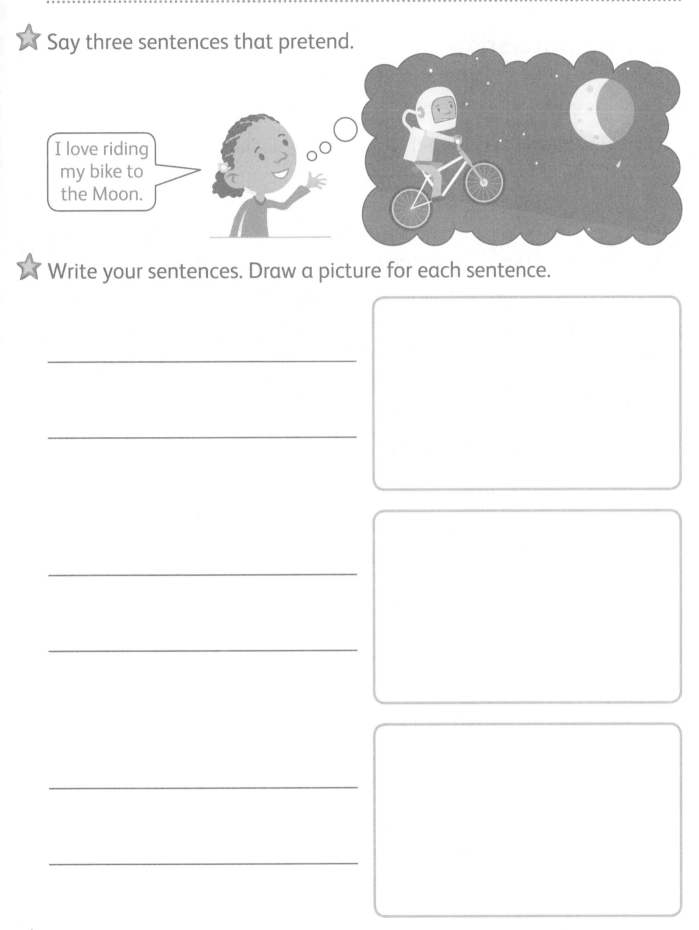

I love riding my bike to the Moon.

⭐ Write your sentences. Draw a picture for each sentence.

⭐ Read your sentences to a friend.

Writing patterns

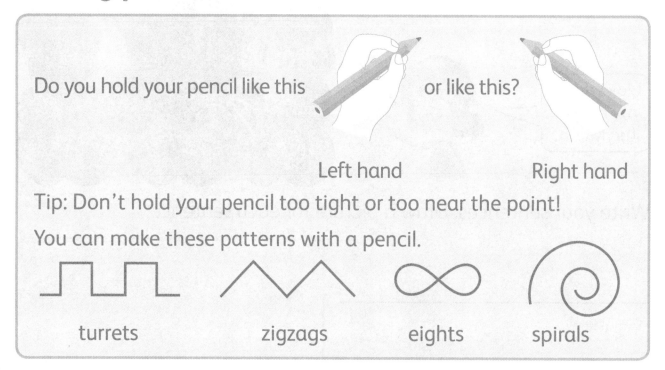

Do you hold your pencil like this   or like this?

          Left hand   Right hand

Tip: Don't hold your pencil too tight or too near the point!

You can make these patterns with a pencil.

turrets   zigzags   eights   spirals

⭐ What patterns can you see in the picture? Tell a friend.

⭐ Draw turrets, zigzags, eights and spirals on the plain things in the picture.

⭐ Trace these patterns with your finger.
Then trace them with your pencil.

⭐ Fill each T-shirt with these patterns.

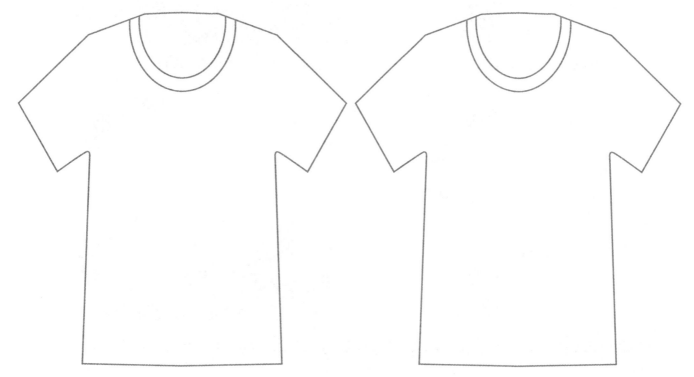

Writing capital letters

Get set to write well:

1. sit up

2. feet down and flat

3. elbows off the table

4. chair legs all down

5. do not hold pencil too tightly

6. pencil down and now begin.

⭐ Look at how to write each capital letter. Trace and then copy.

A   B   C   D   E

F   G   H   I   J

K   L   M   N   O

P   Q   R   S   T

U   V   W

X   Y   Z

When we write names, we begin the name with a capital letter.

Lan Lok Asha Zain Sol Cayo

⭐ Write your name. Circle the capital letter.

⭐ Write the names of three friends on these scarves. Begin each name with a capital letter.

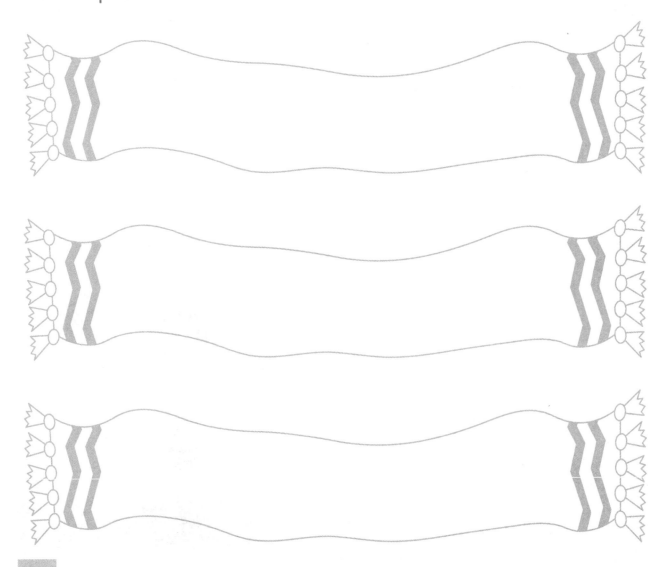

Circle the names. Copy each sentence, adding capital letters for the names.

asha and sol are looking at a nest.

_____

_____

zain is jumping and cayo is splashing.

_____

_____

hikmat and iffat are rolling down the hill.

_____

_____

 Now write a sentence about you and two friends. Write their names.

_____

_____

Writing sentences

When we write words together that make sense, we write in sentences.

A sentence needs a capital letter at the start and a full stop at the end.

The goat has floppy ears.

Its name is **Ben.**

 Copy each sentence, adding capital letters and full stops.

we are going to the zoo with Ian and Iok

_____

_____

i am going to the Moon in this box with zain

_____

_____

i am a famous footballer and my name is victor

_____

_____

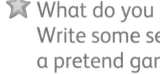 What do you like to pretend? Write some sentences about a pretend game here.

Read your sentences. Check you have used a capital letter at the start and a full stop at the end of each sentence.

_____

_____

_____

_____

What can you remember?

 Read and draw.

Draw a big brown

Draw a little red

 Circle the odd one out.

Tip: What sort of voice are these children using? Loud or soft?

Why is it the odd one out?

_____

 Say the name of each animal.
Join the pairs that have the same sound at the start.

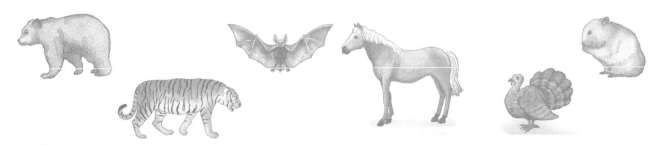

Name each picture. What letter sound is the same in each?
Write the letters.

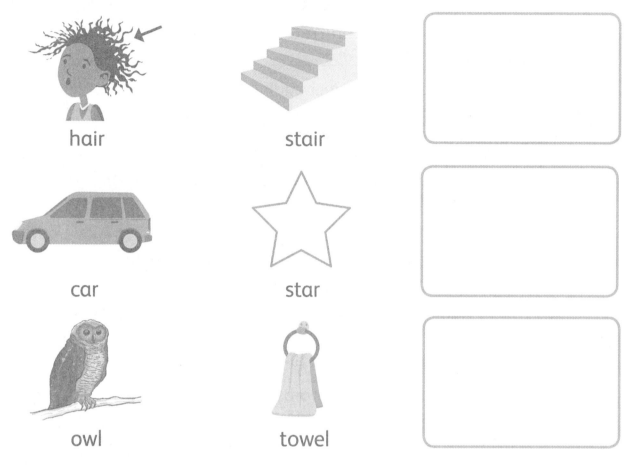

hair   stair

car   star

owl   towel

 Write the words for these pictures.

_____   _____   _____

 Write your name. Add the capital letters and a full stop.

My name is _____

Self-assessment

Colour the stars to show what you can do!

Understanding, listening and speaking	I can sequence and retell sentences in stories and events.	☆
	I can find the correct ending to a story.	☆
	I can ask *how* questions.	☆
Exploring words	I can learn and use new words about animals.	☆
	I can describe how things look.	☆
	I can talk about things that may happen in the future.	☆
Tuning in to sounds and voice	I can explain when we use different voices and why.	☆
	I can use my voice in different ways.	☆
	I can hear and say words that begin with the same sound.	☆
Letters and sounds 3	I can spot phonemes that have two or three letters, like *or* and *air*.	☆
	I can read and spell words that have two consonants at the beginning or end.	☆
	I can read and write some tricky words.	☆
Reading stories that pretend	I can sort stories into real or pretend.	☆
	I can choose or make up story endings.	☆
	I can read sentences and match them to pictures.	☆
Writing	I can copy and write patterns: turrets, zigzags, eights and spirals.	☆
	I can write capital letters in the correct way.	☆
	I can write capital letters for names.	☆
	I can write sentences with a capital letter and a full stop.	☆